The Worldview Series

Empowered by
Clarity

ALI NAJI

THE MAINSTAY
FOUNDATION

By: The Mainstay Foundation

Printed in the United States.

ISBN: 978-1943393367

In the name of *what is true*, including *what is right*, I offer the following reflections to any and every reasonable thinker seeking clarity. Be empowered and share the light. But this is only the beginning.

CONTENTS

EMPOWERED BY CLARITY

Acknowledgements

In writing this short booklet, I considered including references to expert thinkers with relevant discussions branching off of the core ideas I invite the reader to reflect on. But I decided that doing so would likely defeat the purpose of this publication. As a conscious reader will notice, although I discuss ideas that can be examined more closely by experts, I intently attempt to elucidate them in a way accessible to the non-expert. This work aims to highlight foundational reflections that are much closer to home than one might initially suspect. These truths, however modest, should be a guiding light in the darkness, never extinguished. Realize that the lights have always been on – we just had to open our eyes and see.

Nevertheless, I realize the significance of being self-aware regarding the influence of multiple factors on my use of language, terms, categories and frameworks.[1] Although truth is out there for any sincere seeker, we seldom journey in a vacuum. For the ensuing reflections, I am thus indebted to various gracious souls, communities, and environments. First and foremost, I thank the truth for being there in a way that is accessible to some extent, regardless of all else. I thank my loving parents, supportive family and reliable friends, especially my beloved wife. I am forever grateful to my mentors and educators. Institutions and communities of learning across time and space command my lasting gratitude and reverence. I extend special appreciation to the Mainstay Foundation and its editorial team for supporting this project. To those I have neglected proper recognition and thanks, I cannot truly do you justice. As the wise have said, "How can I truly thank you when being able to say, 'thank you,' calls for another, 'thank you'?"[2] Any good in my work is yours and the shortcomings are all my own.

Foundations

These seven reflections are keys to clarity on a multitude of questions that a person faces in the voyage home. I have personally formulated my worldview and addressed objections to it in light of these fundamental principles. As simple as they may appear at face value, they have the propensity to resolve quagmires that have paralyzed even experts in their fields. Let us not forget that sometimes attention to detail keeps us from seeing the bigger picture. We may lose touch with obvious facts when we get caught up in specialization. This booklet brings to the surface what many would find to be unspoken assumptions of reasonable thinking. It is a reminder and an invitation to be empowered. The coming booklets in this series will take these reflections as sound assumptions.

First: Truth does not Require Agreement

1+1=2, regardless whether we happen to agree to it or not. Right? But there are different reasons why individuals may disagree on issues so elementary. Sure, when I read "1+1=2" I picture numbers, but another person may have never learned the meaning of these symbols. In other words, we may not always be speaking the same language. At other times, we may be speaking the same language – English let's say – but we are still not *speaking the same language*. What I mean is that

each of us has a complicated set of ideas that sur-
rounds and meshes with our thought processes. At
times our diverse experiences, personalities, pref-
erences, etc... all create a unique web of thoughts
that can challenge our agreement on terms, even if
we're all speaking in English. It's also possible that
we may wake up on the wrong side of the bed one
morning. Maybe I haven't had a proper breakfast.
Maybe my mind is cluttered with the loads of re-
sponsibilities weighing on my shoulders... Or
maybe we're each looking at things from a very
different perspective when we would have otherwise agreed.

Or, perhaps, there is no issue with the idea on its
own merit – we may secretly agree – but one of us
is holding out for some reason! Admitting the truth
is not always easy. After all these hours (or even
years!) of studying, publishing, debating, etc... how
can I admit that I was simply mistaken? That does
not only go for admitting to others by the way. I
can't be wrong, I can't be – right? Sometimes it
may be difficult to admit the truth even to oneself.
Intuitively, though, it seems generally more difficult to fool myself than to fool others. Despite that
inkling of guilt and core sense of responsibility to

the truth, I can conveniently choose to sweep what I know under the rug and hope that no one will notice. I may know that a certain proposition (such as 1+1=2) is true, but there is so much at stake in admitting it! So we may not always agree – at least we won't admit it all the time. The thought exercise here aims to bring to the forefront of the reader's mind a number of fundamental truths. Some things are true, regardless whether others agree on them being true or not. Sure, issues that are so powerfully evident should have the propensity to impose themselves on a sound mind and conscience. But so many factors, such as the ones referred to here, can stand in the way. *The bottom line is that the light of what is right illuminates the darkness – regardless whether others are looking the other way or choose to close their eyes or have any other impairment impacting their vision.*

Second: Awareness Comes in Many Forms

As I type these words, I realize that I do not have to look at the keyboard. My fingers just seem to know where to locate the next letter I would like to type. If you were to ask me to draw the keyboard layout from memory, however, I probably would have a hard time doing so. For me to articulate what I know, in this case, is difficult. I can show you as I type that I do know where the keys are but it is not nearly as easy for me to explain in words. *Knowing is one thing and being able to articulate what I know is another.*[3] Sometimes I *am* aware of things, but only in a way that I cannot necessarily articulate with ease. This is an example of how awareness comes in more than one form.

Feeling hungry is not the same as *remembering* that feeling. Actually experiencing joy is very different than recalling or imagining the mere meaning. Sensing the impact of the cool breeze is one thing and being told about it is another. No matter how poetic a description of honey's sweetness can be, it does not cut it - tasting the sweetness of honey is a distinct experience. These are different examples that illustrate how awareness comes in many forms. In the world of communication, we typically deal with concepts – ideas, recollections, reflections of truths. But even more profoundly close to home is the awareness each of us experiences individually when we *sense*, when we *feel*, when we *taste*, when we are *aware*. The latter form is present in a way that cannot be mistaken or doubted because it is a direct experience of reality. So there are at least two forms of awareness related to reality that we can discern: (1) direct experience of reality (sometimes called *knowledge by presence*); and (2) concepts about reality – or plainly, conceptual knowledge;

Direct Experience of Reality

I can feel it when I am satisfied. I directly experience my inner strength. I can similarly sense my core weaknesses and deficiencies. I sense the experiencing "I" when I write, "*I* feel the flow of energy powering me up at every moment." I feel my own presence that is. I experience – without any intermediary – my knowledge, my conviction, my love, and my resolve. When I am sad, I feel it without asking for validation. When I am hungry, I know it without need for investigation (except maybe to find some food). If someone were to tell me, then, "Maybe you are not hungry, maybe you just think you are!" I would find it amusing that someone could even entertain such a doubt. I am feeling it directly, there is no room for doubt! Not only is this experience true because it is so vividly presents itself, it is true because it is the reality in question itself – not merely a reflection.

Conceptual Knowledge of Reality

Granted, tasting honey is not the same as hearing about it. But a description of honey can be accurate, nonetheless. I do not have to journey to the Grand Canyon to know a thing or two about it. I do not have to be depressed myself to know that it is a difficult condition. I do not have to see a miracle myself to understand what it means and the power it can have. Although our knowledge can be traced back (in one form or another) to direct experiences, much of our access to reality is *indirect* – through concepts.

Indirect access means that we see *reflections* of reality – either accurate or inaccurate/fuzzy ones. I'll refer to the mirror analogy[4] later. If concepts are windows, then we usually look at reality through the glass. Things can cloud our vision but they don't always cloud our vision. Otherwise, there would have been no *window* to begin with. Knowledge is only knowledge to the extent that it is a clear window to reality, a clean mirror reflecting things as they truly are. For the remainder of this booklet, when I refer to knowledge, I mean conceptual knowledge – indirect access to reality.

In order to be clear on what we *know* as opposed to what we merely *think* we know, we first need to realize that *not all truths are created equal*. That is what the next section discusses.

Third: Not all Truths are Created Equal

The Self-evident Coin

Right off the bat, some things just do not add up. To say, "This statement is both true and false – in the same exact sense – at the same time" does not add up. Similarly evident would be the falsehood in the claim that, "Nothing is certain," or that, "No proposition is universal," or that, "No absolute truth exists." For each of these statements cannot hold its ground without belying itself! (If *nothing is certain* then we cannot be certain about *nothing being certain*; If no proposition is universal then this proposition cannot apply universally; if no absolute truth exists then this claim cannot be true in an absolute sense).

On the flipside of the same *self-evident* "coin", some things do add up! "I know some things," and, "That means: (1) I exist; (2) some things exist; and (3) my knowledge of some things exists." Our most foundational information is represented by this self-evident coin – whatever we know builds off of this self-evident coin at the most basic level. This includes not only the data one gets through the five senses. It includes the elementary principles that allow me to make sense of experimental data. "This just happened. *Something must explain it, unless it is self-explanatory.*" The self-evident coin represents not only my knowledge that I felt hunger, fear, or happiness a few moments ago, but also my basic moral maxims that *what is right ought to be done* and *what is wrong ought to be avoided.* "If you give me a choice between doing what is right and doing what is wrong, with all things equal (i.e. If I were to be given the same monetary or social reward either way), *choosing to do what is right is a no-brainer.*" "Justice should be served. Injustice is wrong."

The self-evident coin represents *infallible* knowledge *so evident that it does not require proof.* "2 is half of 4. That's obvious. How can I prove it? Well, 1 is half of 2. That's clear enough right? And 4 = 2 + 2. So half of 4 = half of 2 + half of 2 = 1 + 1 = 2." In some cases, however, the knowledge the self-evident coin includes is already *so intensely luminous that nothing else can shed further light on it*. For instance, how can I prove that *two ends of a contradiction cannot both be true*? Good luck trying. Nonetheless, it is no less evident. Rather, the integrity of knowledge depends on this fact that when something is true it is not false, and when it is false it is not true.

Currency Requiring Further Calculations

Yet, there are other things that we're not sure about at first glance – they require further calculation, thinking and perhaps even extended research. This includes all conceptual knowledge not represented by the self-evident coin described earlier. Such a broad category of knowledge includes: **(1) matters requiring *expert* research, such as a jurist's knowledge of law-derivation or a surgeon's medical knowledge**; and **(2) matters *not requiring* experts but requiring generally reasonable, careful consideration**, such as a reflective individual's answers to some key worldview questions (e.g. Where did I come from? Where am I going? And how do I get there safely?).

Experts reign only in the realm of matters requiring expert research. In that domain, sound reasoning has me defer to the specialist to the extent demanded by the issue at hand. If I have a potentially life-threatening illness, I will not be caught dead attempting to diagnose and treat myself haphazardly when I have access to an expert physician. Reasonble devotees of a spiritual way of life would not risk harming their spiritual health by blindly following their forefathers instead of referring to the expert research of the most qualified specialist(s) on the right path. *Yet, if the matter at hand is not one requiring expert research, if the issue can be adequately calculated by a reasonable non-special-*

ist, let alone if the question belongs to the self-evident coin, then the expert can sit this one out. In fact, if a so-called "specialist" attempts to address such questions and comes up with some skeptical answers that contradict sound reason, then that "specialist" opinion is bankrupt. I do not submit to an expert in everything. I only submit to an expert in matters that require expertise. "I know how to deal with the common cold. I know how to change a tire. I know that justice should be served. I know that nothing comes from nothing. I know that everything requires an explanation unless it has what it takes to be self-explanatory."

Fourth: A Mirror is a Mirror

There are two ways to look at a mirror:

1. to look at it as an object among other objects in a room; and
2. to look into the mirror and see the reflection it displays.

The first way of looking at the mirror is similar to the way we would look at the couch, the fan, the door, etc... Nothing particularly distinct here. Sure, looking at the mirror this way helps us identify where the mirror was made, what shape and size the mirror has, and how it is situated in the room. But it is the second way of looking at the mirror that shows us what makes a mirror *a mirror*. *This second way of looking at the mirror is what concerns us regarding the nature of knowledge; it is the reflection dimension.*

Bring a rose in front of a mirror and it is in some way reflected on the mirror's surface. Of course, there must be sufficient light in the room for us to see the rose, let alone its reflection. As long as the mirror is clean enough to be called a mirror, to act in that capacity for which it is called a mirror, then the rose's image is imprinted on the mirror. Notice that the mirror could have been made in the East, the West, or in a different galaxy, and it would not make a difference from the aspect of its function as a mirror. If it did make a considerable difference then there would be no mirror – it would be something else. Sure, I can ask, "Where was this mirror made?" I can think, "This mirror's history is worthy of examination. We can learn about the place of its origin by examining its features." The likes of these questions come with their own utility. That's great. But the key takeaway from this analogy is that the mirror still reflects the rose – more or less.

All other factors cannot change that fact. Or else, there was no mirror to begin with.

At least some of our knowledge is like the rose reflected on the mirror. Regardless where we come from and when we happen to make our mark in this world, if we have any knowledge at all then there remains a level – however modest – at which we have a *mirror of sorts* reflecting reality. So long as we know anything, we have a mirror reflecting something about the reality outside of ourselves. The point of emphasis here is that I can acknowledge how history and location can have a role to play in my existence without doubting the obvious – I still have a *mirror* and much of what I see is clearly true.

Fifth: Knowledge is not a Symbol

For a symbol to have meaning to us, we have to have prior knowledge of: (1) the symbolic representation (e.g. the word "cat"); (2) the meaning being symbolized (e.g. that little furry, carnivorous mammal); and (3) the relationship between those two things. Once we have these three pieces of prior knowledge, only then does the symbol "cat" have meaning in my mind. That's why I don't understand Chinese yet! If you understand Chinese, that's because you've already become familiar with those three layers of prior knowledge. Why don't I understand a cardiogram result when it is presented to me? Because I have not been adequately trained to read it. I do not have the prior knowledge of the curvy lines, what they precisely represent, and the relationship between the two. But a physician with the know-how does find meaning in those symbols.

Notice how a prior level of *knowledge* is required. A painting is the same as any other symbol in this regard. So is a statue. If I do not have knowledge of (1) the painting/photograph/statue; (2) who it represents (due to resemblance, for instance); and (3) the relationship between the two; then I will not think of Abraham Lincoln when I see the Lincoln Memorial. A symbol (whether it be a line, a photograph, a painting, a statue, or any other form) is one thing while knowledge is another. A symbol depends on a prior level of knowledge. Hence, knowledge comes first. Any attempt to explain knowledge must not be reduced to a symbol. In other words, knowledge cannot be reduced to chemical signals, for example. Those are merely symbols – rid of meaning if not for a prior level of *knowledge*. For the same reason, knowledge is not a map of electric activity. Those may be symbols representing activity related to knowledge but they cannot explain knowledge itself. Why? Because *knowledge is not a symbol*. Knowledge – so long as it is knowledge – is a reflection of reality, a window allowing us to peek into reality.

Sixth: Not Knowing does not Justify Rejecting

Is there intelligent life in the universe? I mean besides human life. If I do not know the answer, does it make sense to reject the possibility right off the bat? *Doesn't rejecting require evidence just as much as accepting?* Maybe the future has in store the evidence I've been looking for. Being reasonable means that I have clarity in this regard. I may not have all the answers now, but I know that *recognizing when I do not know* is necessary progress on the path of *coming to know*.

If I am under the impression that an individual can only gain one Bachelor's degree in a lifetime, then I will have a hard time explaining how: (1) John has a Bachelor's degree in Engineering; and (2) John also has a Bachelor's degree in Philosophy. But I see the transcript in front of me. (1) is true and (2) is true. How do I explain these facts? Each of them is true on its own merit – that much is clear. Yet, I may be reluctant to submit to that reality because I am under the impression that an individual can only gain one Bachelor's degree at any given time. Should I doubt (1) or (2)? Or both? Am I justified in doing so? If I am sure of (1) and I am sure of (2) then how can I even consider doubting either? Of course, we all know the problem arises because of the assumption that a person cannot have two Bachelor's degrees at once. But the strategic problem is even more profound: *doubting what I know to be true*. Not being able to explain all my knowledge in a unified *theory of everything* right now does not justify *doubting* – let alone *rejecting* – what I already *know* to be true. What's true is true. What's false is false.

If: (1) I see Mary at the library reading; and, (2) when I peek out the window, I see a virtually identical resemblance to Mary walking by; then I may be taken aback for a moment. I know (1) to be true without a doubt. I also know (2) to be true. If I have never considered the possibility that Mary has a twin sister, I may be tempted to doubt my knowledge. But that would be flawed for many reasons. Most fundamentally, it would be flawed because to doubt what I know for sure is absurd. Not being able to explain all my information in one holistic account does not change the truth of what I already know. My inability to explain how the two facts can be reconciled may be overcome in the future. It goes without saying that this is all assuming I know (1) and (2) without a doubt. If I am unsure of (1) or of (2) then that would call for an entirely different discussion.

When I do not have knowledge about something in question, as I discussed in the beginning of this section, what is the sensible position to take? Simply not to reject? That is definitely part of a sound approach. But should I stop there? Imagine I am on a train to the airport. I've left early because I want to be sure not to miss my flight. I've packed all my things carefully but I am still thinking back to make sure I didn't miss anything important... Then it hits me, "I may have forgotten my laptop!" I am not sure though. It may be in my suitcase. It is most likely the case that I have not forgotten it. How could I have forgotten something so important when I made sure to double check what I packed before leaving home? Still, the laptop is a crucial tool for my work and my productivity partially relies on it. I can use it to read and type on the train, plane and pretty much wherever I go. I am willing to go back home and pick it up. That is how important it is. So what's the first thing I do? To avoid the serious inconvenience of lacking my laptop, I open up my luggage and look for it. It made the most sense for me to do so despite only going off of a possibility – albeit one of serious consequences for me. *The percentage of chance I take into consideration is of little significance when I consider the potential repercussions at stake. Avoiding serious danger takes precedence.*

When it comes to the questions of serious stakes in life, being reasonable drives me to gain clarity and become certain. If for some reason I fail to achieve absolute certainty, I am still determined to be sure beyond reasonable doubt. I may have to compare different scenarios, competing interpretations and rivaling outlooks. *Ultimately, the consequences involved push me to take the safest position on the issue at hand, in light of the evidence available to me.* That goes for my thinking as well as my relevant course of action. This is the invitation of reasonable clarity.

Seventh: Knowledge without Action is at Risk

I may know that smoking is harmful to me, but I cannot bring myself to admit it deep within, let alone utter it out loud. I may, thus, be much less willing to actually quit smoking. I may be well-aware that a dead corpse can do me no real harm (despite all the mummy movies I've seen), but how willing am I to take a stroll in a graveyard at night? Knowing that killing is wrong does not keep a murderer from carrying out atrocities. Knowing that we would not want ill done to us does not always keep us from doing ill to others. Knowing is one thing and submitting – at heart and in action – to what I know is another. Recognizing this, I must also become clear with myself on when I fall short of submitting to what I know and I must consider the potential side effects of those shortcomings.

Knowing little is still knowing. And I know that knowing comes with responsibility. I may not know much but I know that doing the right thing is the right way to go. It is a worthy pursuit in and of itself. It is about standing for what is right. It also keeps me sane as a thinker of sound judgment. This is not only about knowing the answers to basic mathematics. This is about knowing that stealing from a helpless person is downright wrong. This is about recognition that the murder of innocents is wrong regardless what a given society says about it. This is about awareness that when I know something I should hold myself accountable for acting wisely in light of that knowledge – that is independent of what others may say or think about it. Others may choose to ignore that candle deep within. Many may attempt to extinguish that flame of what is right by ignoring it, by burying it, by trying to silence it. But we cannot. Not after the truth we now see and the call that we now hear. I must search if I do not know. I must investigate. I have a responsibility to the truth, however little of it I now know. I am held accountable by my very own soul and I can see my current state with piercing insight. I know what I know and I know that there is still much to learn. Challenging tyranny, standing in the face of injustice, with wisdom and forbearance – these are things I know to be right. I know that searching for answers when I do not have them is the sound approach. Recognizing my limits and transcending them only through fair means is another thing that I know.

If I do not act on this knowledge then I risk succumbing to the fate that so many others have faced. The heartless, the soulless, and the ignorant have chosen to forget or have chosen to bury the priceless gem that lies within. They have doubted the most obvious of truths. They have abandoned the clearest paths of rectitude. They have turned every pursuit into one of materialistic interest. They have lost the value of friendship for its own sake. They have missed the point of what doing the right thing means. The invitation to clarity is a call to being sound of judgment. Those of sound judgment aim to see the truth, including what is right to do, no matter how little, and choose to act accordingly. Straying from doing what I know to be right puts my sense of sound judgment at risk. When I expose the precious gem to the elements without proper protection, when I leave it unappreciated and unattended, when I throw it under a bus... I risk its destruction. I risk losing it. And if I still have it, it may become so blemished in my crooked vision that I no longer see its charming beauty.

This is an invitation to what is true and what is right to do. This is a declaration of clarity and a stand for those of sound judgment. The same clarity showing me the truth – with or without need for further calculation – shows me what is right to do (even if only a basic level). Acting in light of this knowledge gives me a fighting chance at higher understanding. This call is not specific to one religion, one philosophy or another. This is an exposition for reasonable minds, a needed reminder for one another. Be empowered, share the message, and know that this is only the beginning.

NOTES

[1] References are particularly due to lectures and works by:

- S. Muḥammad Ḥusayn al-Ṭabāṭabāʾī
- Sh. Murtaḍá al-Muṭahharī
- S. Muḥammad Bāqir al-Ṣadr
- Sh. Ghulām Riḍā al-Fayyāḍī
- Sh. Nāṣir Makārim al-Shīrāzī
- Sh. Jaʿfar al-Subḥānī
- S. Jaʿfar al-Ḥakīm
- S. Munīr al-Khabbāz
- S. Muḥammad Bāqir al-Sīstānī
- S. Muḥammad ʿAlī Baḥr al-ʿulūm
- S. Sāmī al-Badrī

- S. Muḥammad Rizvī

[2] Attributed to ʿAlī ibn al-Ḥusayn, known as Zayn al-ʿābidīn, Munājāt al-Shākirīn

[3] This point might be discussed separately but I included it in this section as an example of differing forms of awareness.

[4] Disclaimer: To be taken with a grain of salt. As with all analogies, this one can bring the idea closer to home in one way, but may distance the idea from home in a multitude of other ways. Proceed with caution.

www.ingramcontent.com/pod-product-compliance
Lightning Source LLC
Chambersburg PA
CBHW022342040426
42449CB00006B/672